Cursive Handwriting

Editor: Carla Hamaguchi
Illustrator: Darcy Tom
Designer/Production: Moonhee Pak/Terri Lamadrid
Cover Designer: Barbara Peterson
Art Director: Tom Cochrane
Project Director: Carolea Williams

Table of Contents

Introduction

Each book in the *Power Practice*™ series contains dozens of ready-to-use activity pages to provide students with skill practice. Use the fun activites to supplement and enhance what you are already teaching in your classroom. Give an activity page to students as independent class work, or send the pages home as homework to reinforce skills taught in class. An answer key is provided for quick reference.

The creative activity pages in *Cursive Handwriting* provide an ideal way for students to enhance their handwriting and practice recognizing and forming capital and lowercase letters. As students complete the activities, they will improve their handwriting as well as review these topics:

• states and capitals
• compound words
• parts of speech
• alphabetical order
• antonyms and synonyms
• habitats
• solar system
• plants

Use these ready-to-go activites to "recharge" skill review and give students the power to succeed!

The Alphabet

Aa   Bb   Cc   Dd

Ee   Ff   Gg   Hh

Ii   Jj   Kk   Ll

Mm   Nn   Oo   Pp

Qq   Rr   Ss   Tt

Uu   Vv   Ww   Xx

Yy   Zz

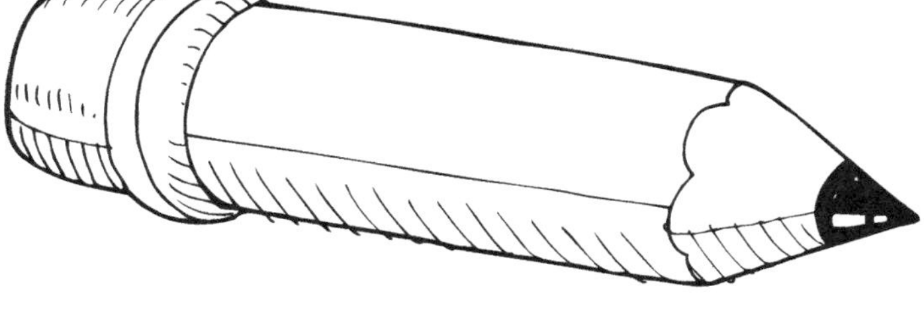

a, d, g

a   *a*   *a*   *a*   *a*   *a*   *a*   *a*   *a*

a

d   *d*   *d*   *d*   *d*   *d*   *d*   *d*   *d*

d

g   *g*   *g*   *g*   *g*   *g*   *g*   *g*   *g*

g

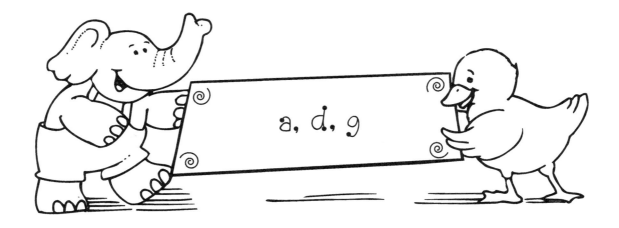

a, d, g

Cursive Handwriting © 2004 Creative Teaching Press

q, o, c

q q q q q q q q q q q q

q

o o o o o o o o o o

o

c c c c c c c c c c

c

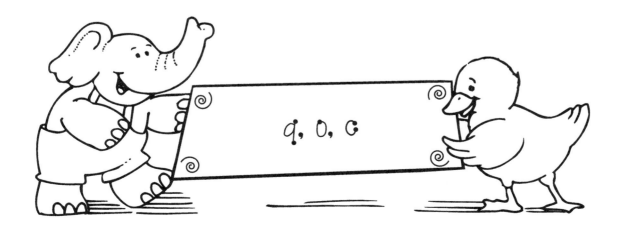

q, o, c

i, t, e

i *i i i i i i i i*

i

t *t t t t t t t t*

t

e *e e e e e e e e*

e

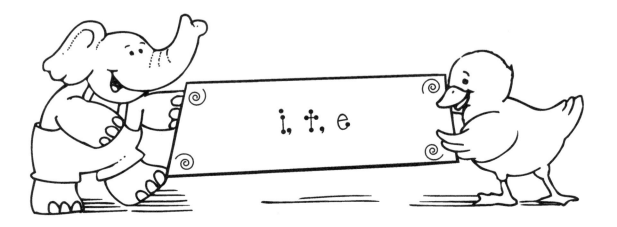

i, t, e

Cursive Handwriting © 2004 Creative Teaching Press

u, w

u 𝓊𝓊 𝓊𝓊 𝓊𝓊 𝓊𝓊 𝓊𝓊 𝓊𝓊 𝓊𝓊

𝓊𝓊

𝓊𝓊

W 𝓌𝓌 𝓌𝓌 𝓌𝓌 𝓌𝓌 𝓌𝓌 𝓌𝓌

𝓌𝓌

𝓌𝓌

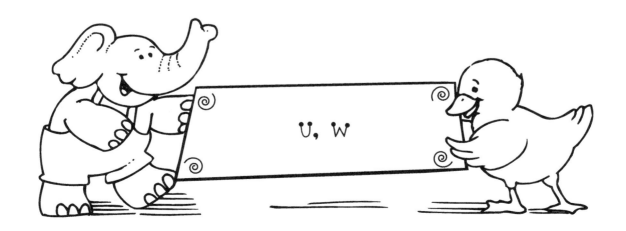

U, w

l, b

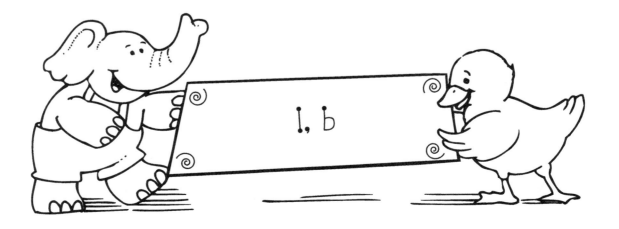

Cursive Handwriting © 2004 Creative Teaching Press

h, k

h | h h h h h h h h h h

h

h

k | k k k k k k k k k k

k

k

h, k

r, s

r   r   r   r   r   r   r   r   r   r

r

r

s   s   s   s   s   s   s   s   s

s

s

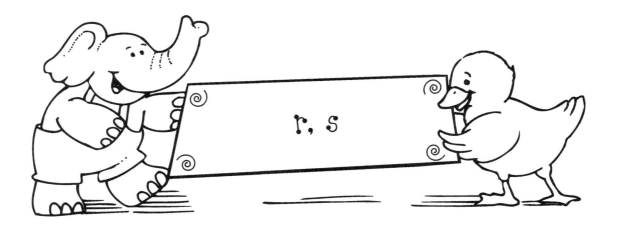

r, s

Cursive Handwriting © 2004 Creative Teaching Press

f, p, j

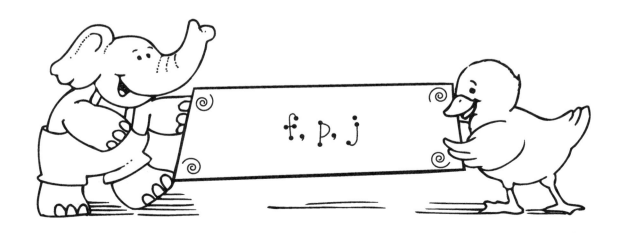

n, m

n *m* *m* *m* *m* *m* *m* *m* *m*

m

m

m *m* *m* *m* *m* *m* *m*

m

m

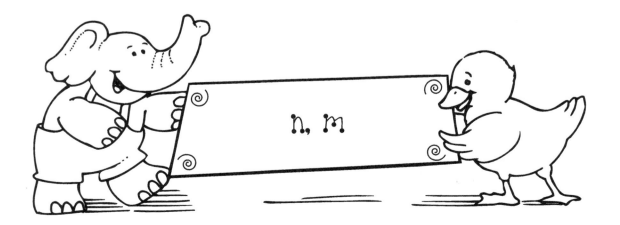

n, m

Cursive Handwriting © 2004 Creative Teaching Press

v, x

V 𝓋 𝓋 𝓋 𝓋 𝓋 𝓋 𝓋 𝓋

𝓋

𝓋

X 𝓍 𝓍 𝓍 𝓍 𝓍 𝓍 𝓍 𝓍

𝓍

𝓍

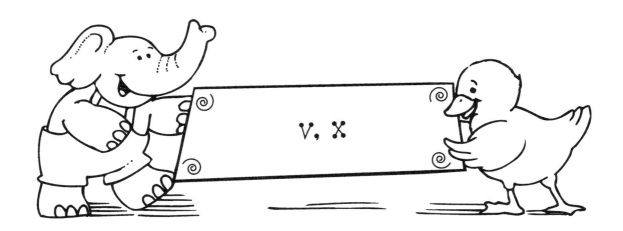

v, x

y, z

y *y* *y* *y* *y* *y* *y* *y* *y*

y

y

z *z* *z* *z* *z* *z* *z* *z*

z

z

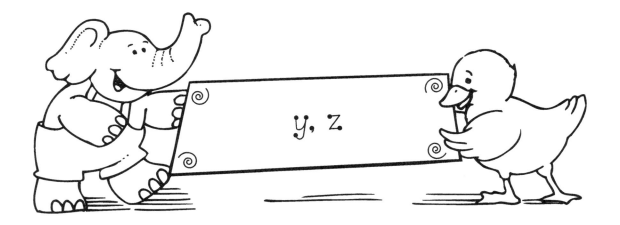

y, z

Cursive Handwriting © 2004 Creative Teaching Press

a-z

a   b   c   d

e   f   g   h

i   j   k   l

m   n   o   p

q   r   s   t

u   v   w   x

y   z

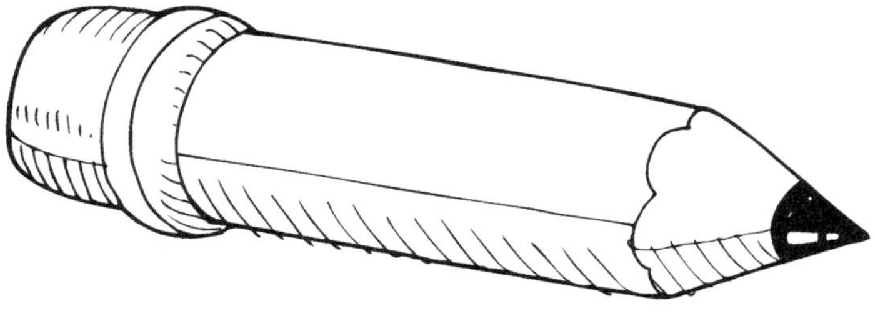

A, D, O

A a *a* *a* *a* *a* *a* *a*

a

D D *D* *D* *D* *D* *D*

D

O O *O* *O* *O* *O* *O*

O

A, D, O

Cursive Handwriting © 2004 Creative Teaching Press

C, E, Q

I, J

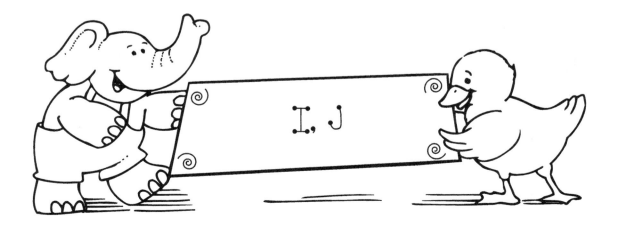

Cursive Handwriting © 2004 Creative Teaching Press

N, M, W

N *n* *n* *n* *n* *n* *n* *n* *n* *n*

n

M *m* *m* *m* *m* *m* *m* *m* *m*

m

W *w* *w* *w* *w* *w* *w* *w*

w

N, M, W

H, K, X

U, Y, V, Z

P, R, B

P P P P P P P P P P P P

P

R R R R R R R R R R R R

R

B B B B B B B B B B B B

B

P, R, B

Cursive Handwriting © 2004 Creative Teaching Press

T, F

G, S, L

Cursive Handwriting © 2004 Creative Teaching Press

A–Z

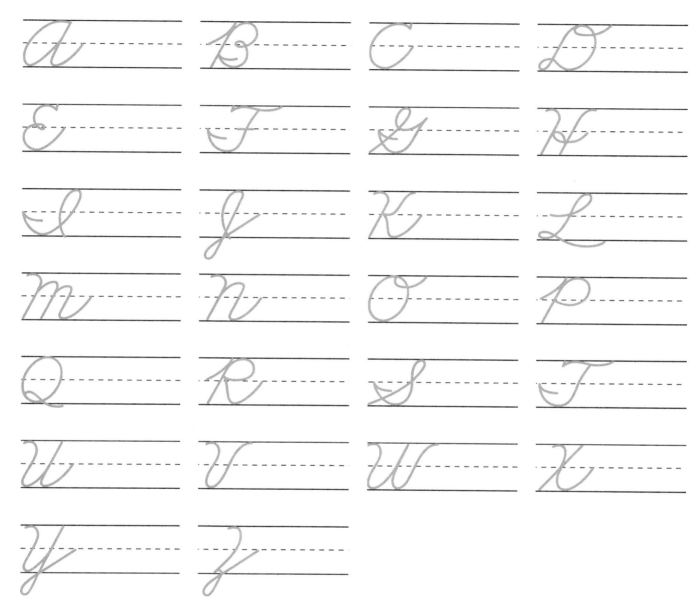

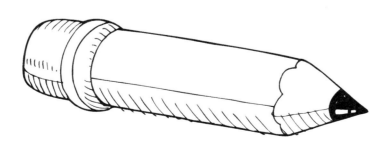

Name _____

alfalfa   Arizona

amount   April

appear   animal

Africa

algebra

almanac

 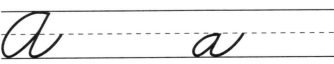

Cursive Handwriting © 2004 Creative Teaching Press

Name ____________________

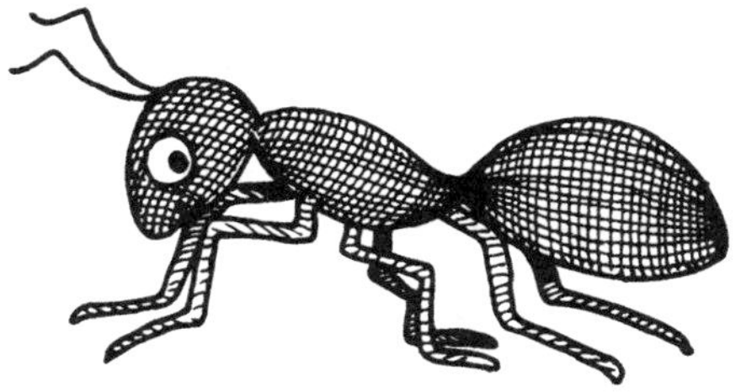

A

A

a

A a

Arnold

apple

An amazing

alligator ate avocados.

Name _____

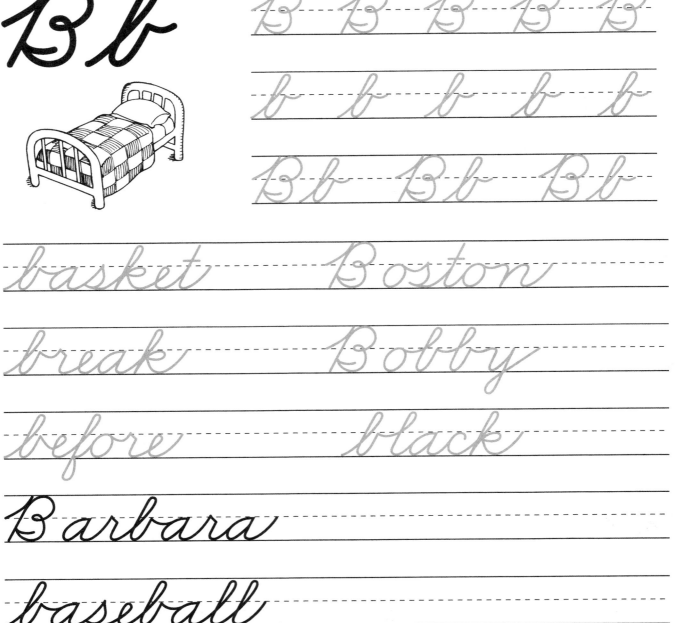

𝓑𝓑   𝓑   𝓑   𝓑   𝓑

𝒷   𝒷   𝒷   𝒷   𝒷

𝓑𝒷   𝓑𝒷   𝓑𝒷

basket   Boston

break   Bobby

before   black

Barbara

baseball

book

Here's my best!

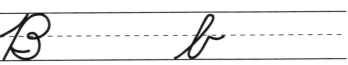

𝓑   𝒷

Cursive Handwriting © 2004 Creative Teaching Press

𝓑

𝓑

𝒷

𝓑𝒷

𝓑𝓇𝒶𝓏𝒾𝓁

𝒷𝒶𝓁𝓁𝑜𝑜𝓃

𝓑𝒾𝑔 𝒷𝓊𝓁𝓁𝒹𝑜𝓏𝑒𝓇𝓈 𝒷𝓁𝑜𝒸𝓀

𝒷𝓊𝓈𝓎 𝒷𝑜𝓊𝓁𝑒𝓋𝒶𝓇𝒹𝓈.

Name _____

Cc

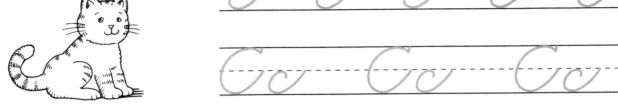

C C C C C

c c c c c

Cc Cc Cc

carrots *Charles*

canyon *child*

China *chocolate*

Catherine

cheese

clown

C c

Cursive Handwriting © 2004 Creative Teaching Press

Name

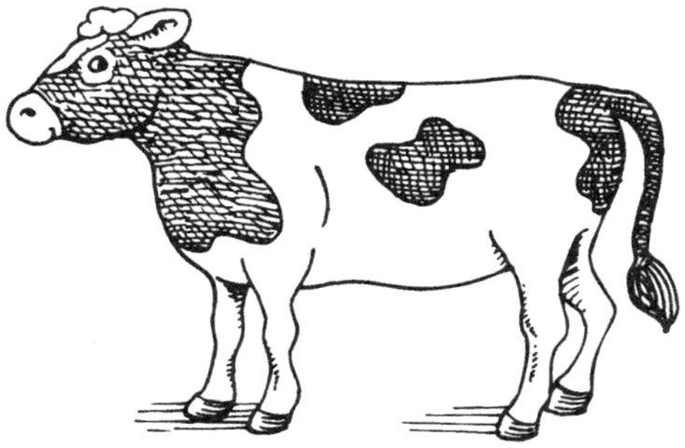

C

C

c

Cc

Columbus

crayon

Colorful costumes

clothed clowns.

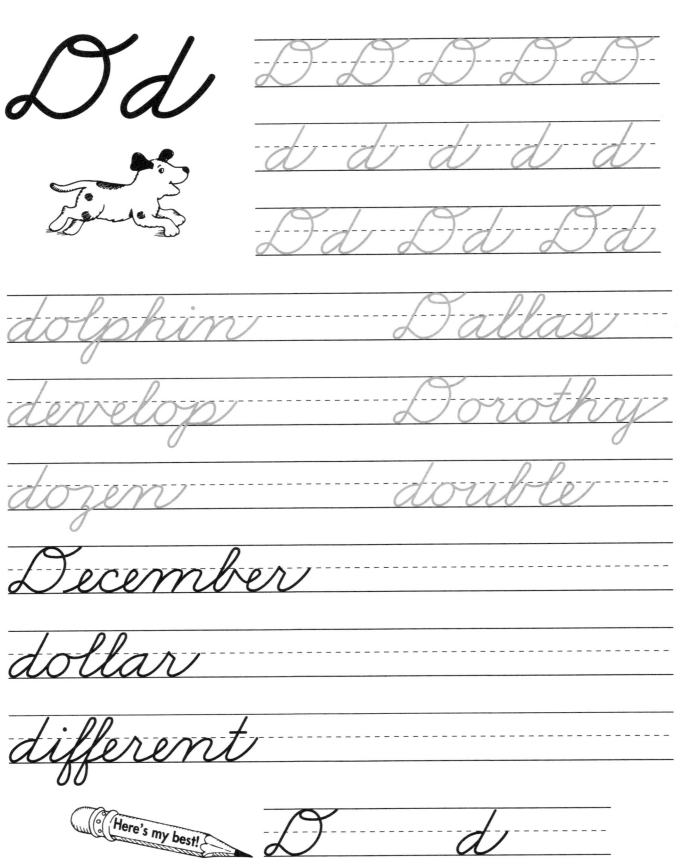

Dd

D D D D D

d d d d d

Dd Dd Dd

dolphin   Dallas

develop   Dorothy

dozen   double

December

dollar

different

Here's my best!   D   d

Cursive Handwriting © 2004 Creative Teaching Press

$\mathcal{D}$

$\mathcal{D}$

d

$\mathcal{D}d$

$\mathcal{D}enver$

$daughter$

$\mathcal{D}affy\ ducks\ drank$

$delicious\ drinks.$

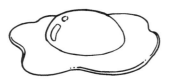

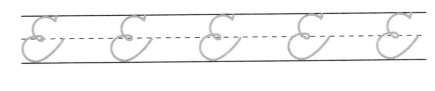

elephant   Ecuador

envelope   Earth

easy   education

Egypt

everyone

enormous

E

E

e

Ee

Europe

example

Everyone enjoys

elegant events.

Cursive Handwriting © 2004 Creative Teaching Press

Ff

friend   France

farm   Florence

flower   famous

Ford

family

football

Here's my best!   *F f*

Cursive Handwriting © 2004 Creative Teaching Press

Name _____

$\mathcal{F}$

$\mathcal{F}$

f

$\mathcal{F}f$

$\mathcal{F}ranklin$

$favorite$

$\mathcal{F}our\ friends\ fed$

$fifteen\ furious\ fish.$

Cursive Handwriting © 2004 Creative Teaching Press

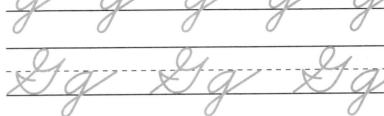

garden   great

glass   Germany

group   Greek

George

geography

giraffe

Cursive Handwriting © 2004 Creative Teaching Press

 G

 G

 g

Gg

Geronimo

grade

Giant gardenias

grow in gardens.

H h

H H H H H

h h h h h h

H h H h H h

hospital   Henry

homework   Hungary

horse   however

Hawaiian

history

honest

Here's my best!   H h

Cursive Handwriting © 2004 Creative Teaching Press

H

H

h

H h

Himalayas

hurricane

Hungry horses had

hot dogs in Holland.

ice cream   Ireland

imagine   Italian

invent   island

India

important

insect

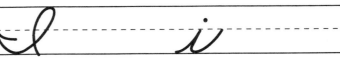

I

I

i

Ii

Inuit

iguana

Ivan invented

invisible ink.

jaguar   Japan

juice   Jordan

joyous   journey

Jonathan

jump

journal

 Here's my best!   J   j

Cursive Handwriting © 2004 Creative Teaching Press

$\mathcal{J}$

$\mathcal{J}$

j

$\mathcal{Jj}$

$\mathcal{Jamaica}$

$jealous$

$jovial\ juveniles$

$juggle\ jars\ of\ jam.$

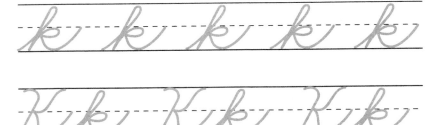

kingdom Korea

knock Kwanzaa

koala know

Kenya

kitchen

kick

Cursive Handwriting © 2004 Creative Teaching Press

K

K

k

Kk

Kennedy

kettle

Kangaroos know

karate kicks.

Cursive Handwriting © 2004 Creative Teaching Press

lettuce   Libya

large   Lansing

listen   lion

Lincoln

language

little

   L   l

Cursive Handwriting © 2004 Creative Teaching Press

Name _____

𝓛

𝓛

𝓵

𝓛𝓵

𝓛atin

library

𝓛arge lazy lions

lick lemons.

Cursive Handwriting © 2004 Creative Teaching Press

Name _____

Mm

m m m m

m m m

Mm Mm

monkey   Malaysia

makes   Madison

medium   mouth

Montreal

math

minute

 Here's my best! M   m

Cursive Handwriting © 2004 Creative Teaching Press

M
M
m

Mm

Mexico

market

Mad monkeys made

many messes.

Name _____

Nn

Nn   n n n n n

n n n n n

Nn Nn Nn

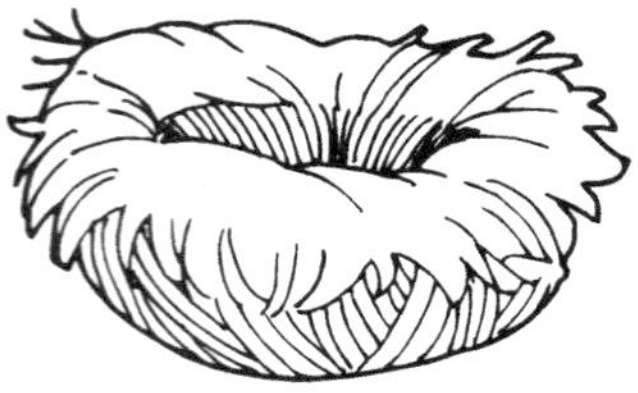

night   Netherlands

noisy   Nixon

normal   number

Norway

nutrition

north

Here's my best!   N   n

Cursive Handwriting © 2004 Creative Teaching Press

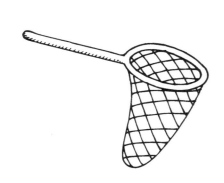

n

n

n

Nn

Nigeria

neighbor

Nine nightingales

nibbled on noodles.

Name _____

Oo

O O O O O

o o o o o

Oo Oo Oo

octopus   Oliver

octagon   Omaha

outdoor   ostrich

Olympics

opera

organize

Here's my best!

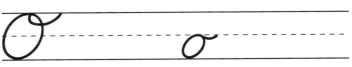

O   o

Cursive Handwriting © 2004 Creative Teaching Press

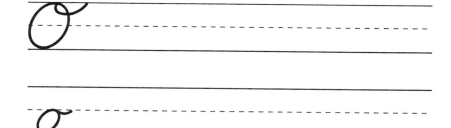

O

O

o

Oo

Ontario

operation

One official offered

old olives.

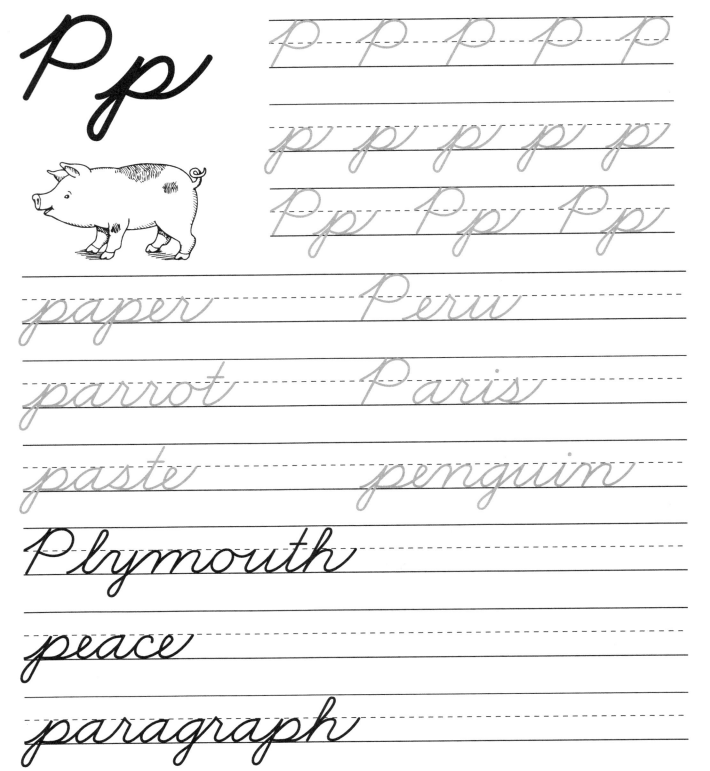

P p

P P P P P P

p p p p p p

Pp Pp Pp Pp

paper   Peru

parrot   Paris

paste   penguin

Plymouth

peace

paragraph

Here's my best!   P   p

Cursive Handwriting © 2004 Creative Teaching Press

Name

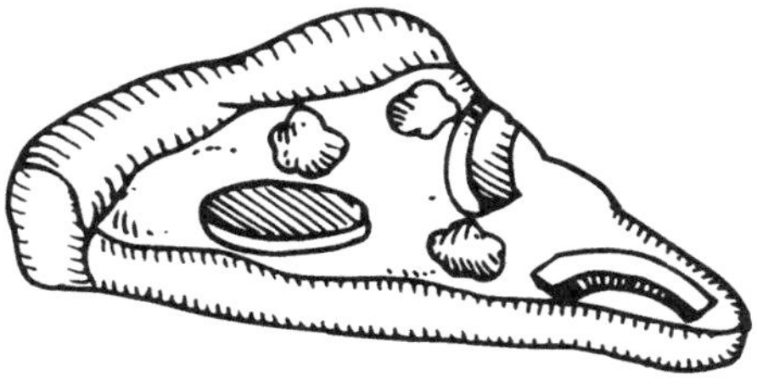

P

P

p

Pp

Poland

president

Patty placed pretty pansies in pots.

Name _____

Qq

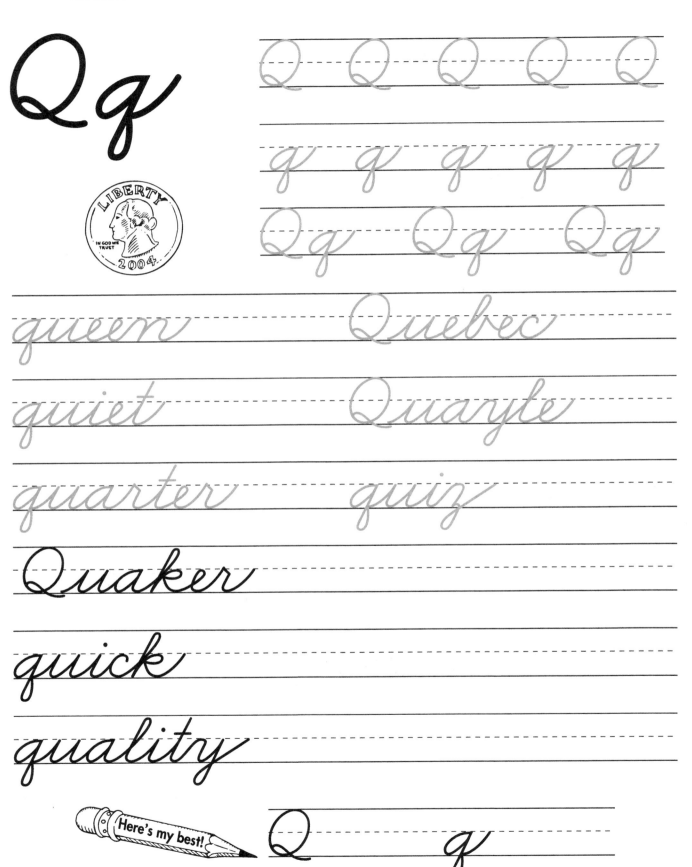

Q Q Q Q Q

q q q q q

Qq Qq Qq

queen   Quebec

quiet   Quayle

quarter   quiz

Quaker

quick

quality

Here's my best!   Q   q

Cursive Handwriting © 2004 Creative Teaching Press

Q

Q

q

Qq

Queensland

question

Queen Ann questioned

the quiet quintuplets.

rabbit   Reagan

radio   Russia

rainbow   reading

Rome

report

rhyme

Cursive Handwriting © 2004 Creative Teaching Press

R

R

r

Rr

Roosevelt

right

The raccoons raced

rapid rabbits.

Name _____

Ss

𝒮 𝒮 𝒮 𝒮 𝒮

𝓈 𝓈 𝓈 𝓈 𝓈

𝒮𝓈 𝒮𝓈 𝒮𝓈

school   Shakespeare

second   Scotland

shine   skate

Sweden

small

soccer

Here's my best!   𝒮   𝓈

Cursive Handwriting © 2004 Creative Teaching Press

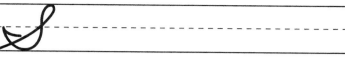

$\mathscr{S}$

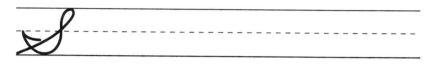

$\mathscr{S}$

$\mathscr{s}$

$\mathscr{S}s$

$Spain$

$special$

$Several\ students$

$sipped\ sour\ soup.$

Tt

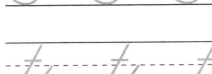

teacher   Tahiti

telephone   Thomas

thumb   terrific

Thailand

tennis

tomato

Cursive Handwriting © 2004 Creative Teaching Press

Name

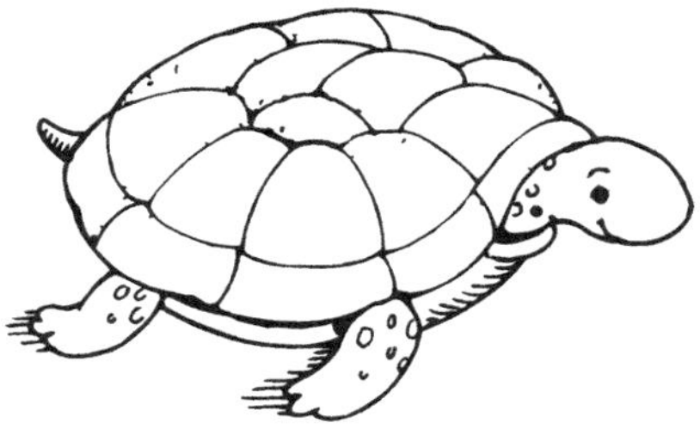

T

T

t

Tt

Tokyo

teeth

Ten tired toucans

traveled to Turkey.

𝒰𝓊

umbrella Uganda

unique Ursula

usually unicorn

Uruguay

useful

uniform

Here's my best!

𝒰   𝓊

Cursive Handwriting © 2004 Creative Teaching Press

$\mathcal{U}$

$\mathcal{U}$

u

$\mathcal{U}u$

$\mathcal{U}kraine$

$under$

$\mathcal{U}ncle\ \mathcal{E}d\ uncovered$

$an\ unusual\ ukulele.$

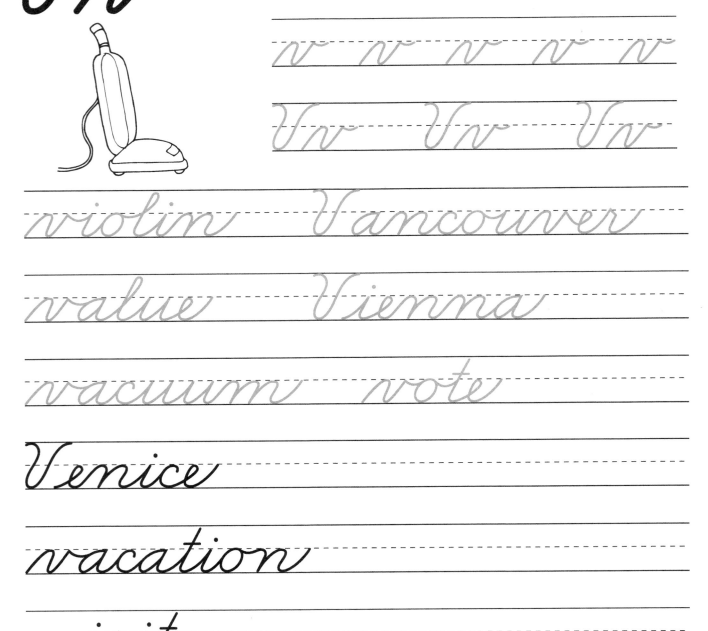

V v

violin   Vancouver

value   Vienna

vacuum   vote

Venice

vacation

visit

Here's my best!   V   v

Cursive Handwriting © 2004 Creative Teaching Press

V
V

v

Vv

Vietnam

variety

Victor's valuable

vases vanished.

Cursive Handwriting © 2004 Creative Teaching Press

Ww

W w W W W W

w w w w w

Ww Ww

warm   Washington

watch   Walter

water   walrus

White House

weather

which

Cursive Handwriting © 2004 Creative Teaching Press

W

W

w

Ww

Winnipeg

writing

William wears

woven western

wear.

X X x

X X X X X

x x x x x

Xx Xx Xx

x-ray   Xhosa

xylophone   Xavier

xenon   xylem

Xanadu

xiphoid

xenia

Here's my best!   X   x

Cursive Handwriting © 2004 Creative Teaching Press

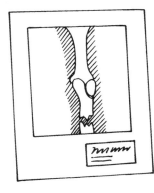

$\mathcal{X}$

$\mathcal{X}$

x

$\mathcal{X}x$

$xebec$

$xylan$

$Xavier\ xeroxed\ the$

$extra\ x\text{-}rays.$

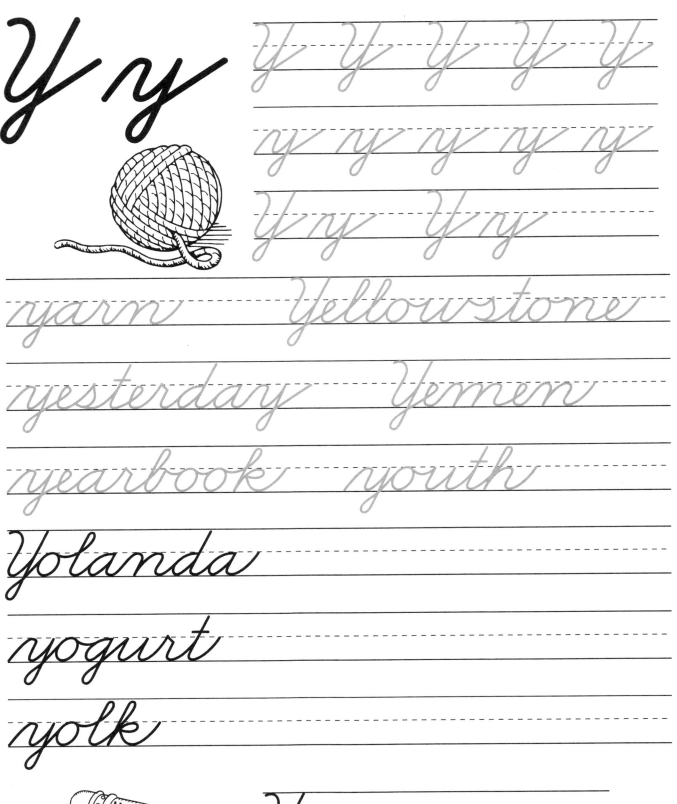

Yy

yarn   Yellowstone

yesterday   Yemen

yearbook   youth

Yolanda

yogurt

yolk

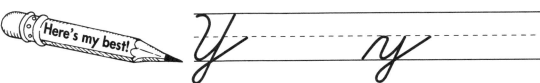

Here's my best!   Y   y

Y

Y

y

Yy

Yosemite

yo-yo

Yesterday yellow

yaks yodelled.

Z Z

Z Z Z Z Z

Z Z Z Z Z

Zz Zz Zz Zz

zebra   *Zaire*

zoo   *Zeus*

zipper   *zinc*

Zimbabwe

zero

zucchini

Here's my best!

Z   *z*

Cursive Handwriting © 2004 Creative Teaching Press

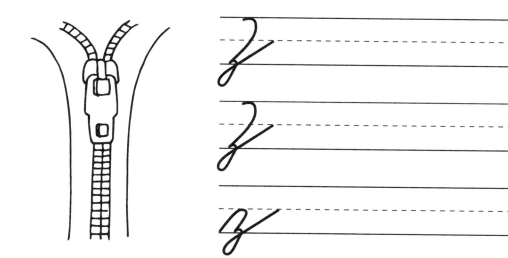

$\mathcal{Z}$

$\mathcal{Z}$

$\mathcal{z}$

$\mathcal{Zz}$

$\mathcal{Zurich}$

$\mathcal{zigzag}$

$\mathcal{Zany\ zebras\ zoom}$

$\mathcal{zealously\ at\ the\ zoo.}$

My Very Best Capital Letters

Write each capital letter in your very best cursive writing.

A B C D E F G H I J K L M N O P Q R S T U V W X Y Z

Cursive Handwriting © 2004 Creative Teaching Press

My Very Best Lowercase Letters

Write each lowercase letter in your very best cursive writing.

a b c d e f g h i j k l m n o p q r s t u v w x y z

Days of the Week

Write the days in the correct order.

Saturday	Monday	Wednesday	Thursday
Tuesday	Friday	Sunday	

Months of the Year

Write each month next to its corresponding abbreviation.

January	April	July	October
February	May	August	November
March	June	September	December

Feb. _____

Oct. _____

Apr. _____

Dec. _____

Sept. _____

May _____

Aug. _____

Mar. _____

Jul. _____

Nov. _____

Jan. _____

Jun. _____

Cursive Handwriting © 2004 Creative Teaching Press

Number Words

Trace and write each number word.

ten

twenty

thirty

forty

fifty

sixty

seventy

eighty

ninety

one hundred

Cursive Handwriting © 2004 Creative Teaching Press

Math Symbols

Write each math term next to its corresponding symbol.

addition	subtraction	multiplication	division
angle	unequal	equals	percent

= ---

+ ---

- ---

X ---

% ---

≠ ---

÷ ---

∠ ---

Name _____

Family

Trace and write each word.

father

mother

brother

sister

grandma

grandpa

cousin

aunt

uncle

daughter

son

Cursive Handwriting © 2004 Creative Teaching Press

Name _____

Proverbs

Copy each proverb.

Better safe than sorry.

- -

Variety is the spice of life.

- -

Nothing succeeds like success.

- -

Don't cry over spilt milk.

- -

All that glitters is not gold.

- -

Continents and Oceans

Write each word.

Asia

Europe

Antarctica

Africa

North America

South America

Australia

Pacific Ocean

Atlantic Ocean

Indian Ocean

Arctic Ocean

States and Capitals

Write each state's name. Then choose the correct capital from the box and write it next to each state.

| Tallahassee | Juneau | Phoenix | Atlanta | Sacramento |
| Dover | Montgomery | Denver | Hartford | Little Rock |

Alabama

Alaska

Arizona

Arkansas

California

Colorado

Connecticut

Delaware

Florida

Georgia

Name _____

States and Capitals

Write each state's name. Then choose the correct capital from the box and write it next to each state.

| Des Moines | Boise | Springfield | Frankfort | Topeka |
| Augusta | Indianapolis | Baton Rouge | Honolulu | Annapolis |

Hawaii

Idaho

Illinois

Indiana

Iowa

Kansas

Kentucky

Louisiana

Maine

Maryland

States and Capitals

Write each state's name. Then choose the correct capital from the box and write it next to each state.

| Carson City | Boston | Helena | Lansing | Trenton |
| Saint Paul | Jackson | Concord | Jefferson City | Lincoln |

Massachusetts

Michigan

Minnesota

Mississippi

Missouri

Montana

Nebraska

Nevada

New Hampshire

New Jersey

States and Capitals

Write each state's name. Then choose the correct capital from the box and write it next to each state.

Salem	Santa Fe	Columbia	Raleigh	Columbus
Oklahoma City	Bismarck	Harrisburg	Albany	Providence

New Mexico

New York

North Carolina

North Dakota

Ohio

Oklahoma

Oregon

Pennsylvania

Rhode Island

South Carolina

Cursive Handwriting © 2004 Creative Teaching Press

Name _____

States and Capitals

Write each state's name. Then choose the correct capital from the box and write it next to each state.

| Cheyenne | Nashville | Charleston | Salt Lake City | Olympia |
| Richmond | Austin | Madison | Montpelier | Pierre |

South Dakota

Tennessee

Texas

Utah

Vermont

Virginia

Washington

West Virginia

Wisconsin

Wyoming

Branches of the
United States Government

The government of the

United States is composed

of three branches: the

executive, the legislative,

and the judicial.

Legislative

The Legislative Branch of
the U.S. government consists
of the Senate, the House of
Representatives, and nine
administrative agencies.

Name _____

Executive

The U.S. Executive Branch consists of the Executive Office of the President, the President's Cabinet, and the independent agencies.

Cursive Handwriting © 2004 Creative Teaching Press

Judicial

The U.S. Judicial Branch consists of the Supreme Court, the highest court of the land; about 95 federal district courts; and 13 federal courts of appeals.

Habitats

A habitat is the place
where a plant or an
animal lives. Five major
habitats are the forest,
grassland, desert, tundra,
and aquatic environments.

Cursive Handwriting © 2004 Creative Teaching Press

Aquatic Habitats

The aquatic habitat is the largest on Earth. Water habitats include ponds, rivers, lakes, wetlands, oceans, tide pools, estuaries, and coral reefs.

Cursive Handwriting © 2004 Creative Teaching Press

Tropical Forests

Tropical forests are near the equator.
All tropical forests receive a large amount
of rainfall. Many different kinds of plants and
animals live in the tropical forest.

Temperate Forests

Temperate forests have cold, wet winters and warm summers. Evergreen and deciduous trees are found in temperate forests.

Boreal Forests

Boreal forests are found in very cold areas. Most of the trees are conifers. The summers are short and the winters are long, cold, and dry.

Deserts

The desert habitats of Earth are harsh places to live. Deserts get less than 20 inches of rain a year. The plants and animals that live in a desert habitat need to be able to store water and withstand the heat.

Tundras

The tundra is the coldest of all habitats. The winter is so long, plants have very little time to grow. Animals use the fat on their bodies to protect them from the cold. The tundra of the arctic has a layer of soil called the permafrost. The permafrost is always frozen.

Grasslands

The grassland habitat has grasses instead of many shrubs or trees. Grasslands have hot, dry summers and short rainy seasons. The savanna, plains, steppe, veldt, and prairies are all examples of grasslands.

Name _____

Plants

Plants are important to life on Earth.
Without plants, there would be no
oxygen to breathe. Plants come in all
shapes and sizes. Trees, shrubs, flowers,
grass, vegetables, and vines are all
types of plants.

Photosynthesis

Most plants make their own food through a process called photosynthesis. Leaves pull up water from the roots and carbon dioxide from the air. Then the water and carbon dioxide mix with energy from the sun to make food for the plant. Photosynthesis also makes a gas called oxygen. We need oxygen to breathe.

Flowering Plants

Daisies, dandelions, pumpkins, and apple trees are all flowering plants. When a plant makes flowers, it is getting ready to produce seeds. Flowers have special parts for making seeds. Flowers come in many shapes, sizes, and colors. The flowers attract insects and birds. They use the nectar as food and help pollinate the flowers.

Cursive Handwriting © 2004 Creative Teaching Press

Name _____

Nonflowering Plants

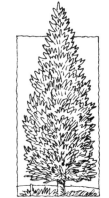

Nonflowering plants do not make flowers. Some, like the conifers, make cones to hold the seeds instead. A pine tree, a cedar tree, and a yew are conifers. Other nonflowering plants do not make seeds. They are called primitive plants. They make new plants with spores. Primitive plants include ferns, moss, and horsetails.

Name _____

Our Solar System

Our solar system is comprised of the Sun and everything that revolves around it, including the nine planets, their moons, and countless asteroids and comets. Although it is huge compared to the planets, the Sun is just an average-size star.

Cursive Handwriting © 2004 Creative Teaching Press

The Sun

The Sun is a large star at the center of our solar system. It is made up of hot gases. All things in our solar system move around the Sun. One full path around the Sun is called a revolution. As the planets move around the Sun, they also spin in circles, or rotate. The time is takes a planet to turn around one time in a circle is called a "day."

The Planets

The four planets closest to the Sun—Mercury, Venus, Earth, and Mars—are small and rocky. The gas giants, Jupiter and Saturn, are huge and lightweight. Uranus and Neptune consist mostly of heavier gases. Pluto and the distant comets are made mostly of ice, and they are relatively small.

Comets and Asteroids

Millions of rocks of all sizes, called
asteroids, revolve around the Sun between
the orbits of Mars and Jupiter in what is called an asteroid
belt. Millions of icy comets orbit the Sun in long ovals. One
of the most famous comets is Halley's Comet, which completes
an orbit of the Sun approximately every 77 years.

Moon Phases

During a period of 29.5 days, the Moon appears to change its shape, or phase. The phase of the Moon depends on where it is in relationship to Earth and the Sun. It grows from new to crescent to gibbous to full in two weeks; then it goes through the cycle in reverse, back to new over the next two weeks.

Solar System Alphabetical Order

Write the words in alphabetical order.

Jupiter	Saturn	Earth	Mars	Venus
Mercury	Uranus	Pluto	Neptune	Sun

Habitats Alphabetical Order

Write the words in alphabetical order.

| desert | marine | forest | grassland | tundra |
| climate | plants | animals | ecosystem | environment |

Plants Alphabetical Order

Write the words in alphabetical order.

| seed | stem | leaf | root | sunlight |
| photosynthesis | water | soil | flower | pollen |

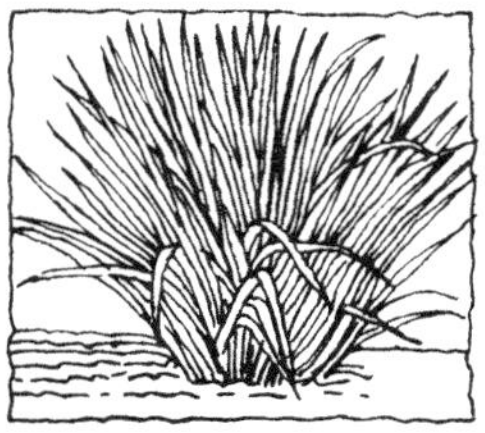

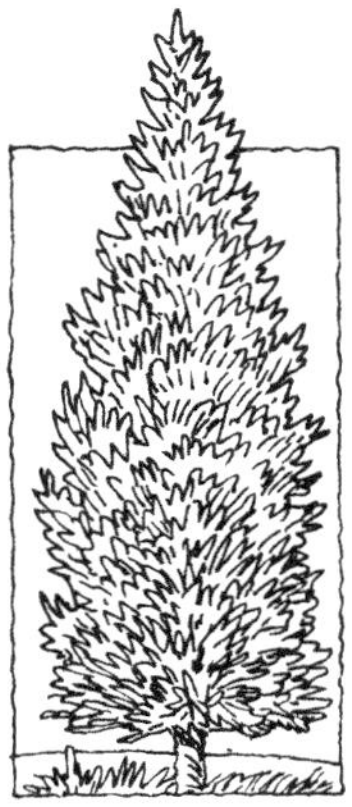

Homophones

Write the sentence that has the correct homophone. Cross out the sentence that has an incorrect homophone.

William **beet** me at checkers.
The Lakers **beat** the Bulls.

I ate the **whole** pie.
She had a **whole** in her jeans.

Mary got her **hair** cut.
Joey has blonde **hare**.

Dogs are not **allowed** in the library.
We were **aloud** to visit my grandma.

She **nose** her multiplication facts.
He **knows** how to ride a bike.

I had to **weight** for the bus.
She had to **wait** for the next train.

Cursive Handwriting © 2004 Creative Teaching Press

Homophones

Write the sentence that has the correct homophone. Cross out the sentence that has an incorrect homophone.

There is a **deer** near the pond.
The **dear** is in the meadow.

I wore my **knew** jeans.
She **knew** the answer to the question.

Please do not **waste** time.
I did not want to **waist** my food.

I went **through** the tunnel.
Billy **through** the ball.

The fish lives in the **sea**.
Whales live in the **see**, too.

Which **rode** should we take?
Tim **rode** his bike to the store.

Cursive Handwriting © 2004 Creative Teaching Press

Compound Words

Choose a word from each box to create a compound word. Write your words below.

moon	wind
bath	table
egg	apple
home	checker
wall	drum

board	stick
room	plant
work	light
spoon	paper
mill	sauce

Cursive Handwriting © 2004 Creative Teaching Press

Compound Words

Choose a word from each box to create a compound word. Write your words below.

brain	black
every	rail
arm	door
out	scare
short	week

body	storm
chair	bell
crow	berry
stop	end
law	road

Name _____

Parts of Speech

Write each word in the correct column.

gasoline	invite	enormous	frighten	ocean
happy	grow	feel	heart	young
jacket	lovely	sister	healthy	wrote
pencil	strange	window	salty	catch
sweep	fancy	student	study	

Nouns   **Verbs**   **Adjectives**

Syllables

Write each word in the correct column.

paragraph	morning	elephant	certain	banana	computer
complete	common	important	dinosaur	almost	telephone
creative	hundred	whether	special	delicious	person

Two Syllables   **Three Syllables**

Cursive Handwriting © 2004 Creative Teaching Press

Syllables

Write each word in the correct column.

vocabulary	activity	magnificent	unnecessary
vegetarian	comprehension	watermelon	electricity
bibliography	communication	opportunity	geography
America	caterpillar	hippopotamus	rhinoceros

Four Syllables   **Five Syllables**

Antonyms

Read each word. Write the antonyms next to each other on the lines.

kind	rare	many	loose	healthy	interior
asleep	whole	common	few	happy	part
tight	awake	exterior	sick	sad	cruel

Cursive Handwriting © 2004 Creative Teaching Press

Synonyms

Read each word. Write the synonyms next to each other on the lines.

easy	mix	whole	fast	assist	smell
gigantic	entire	timid	shy	simple	enormous
odor	help	quick	real	blend	genuine

Answer Key

Days of the Week (page 82)

Sunday
Monday
Tuesday
Wednesday
Thursday
Friday
Saturday

Months of the Year (page 83)

Feb.—February
Oct.—October
Apr.—April
Dec.—December
Sept.—September
May—May
Aug.—August
Mar.—March
Jul.—July
Nov.—November
Jan.—January
Jun.—June

Math Symbols (page 85)

=   equals
+   addition
−   subtraction
×   multiplication
%   percent
≠   unequal
÷   division
∠   angle

States and Capitals (page 89)

Alabama—Montgomery
Alaska—Juneau
Arizona—Phoenix
Arkansas—Little Rock
California—Sacramento
Colorado—Denver
Connecticut—Hartford
Delaware—Dover
Florida—Tallahassee
Georgia—Atlanta

States and Capitals (page 90)

Hawaii—Honolulu
Idaho—Boise
Illinois—Springfield
Indiana—Indianapolis
Iowa—Des Moines
Kansas—Topeka
Kentucky—Frankfort
Louisiana—Baton Rouge
Maine—Augusta
Maryland—Annapolis

States and Capitals (page 91)

Massachusetts—Boston
Michigan—Lansing
Minnesota—Saint Paul
Mississippi—Jackson
Missouri—Jefferson City
Montana—Helena
Nebraska—Lincoln
Nevada—Carson City
New Hampshire—Concord
New Jersey— Trenton

States and Capitals (page 92)

New Mexico—Santa Fe
New York—Albany
North Carolina—Raleigh
North Dakota—Bismarck
Ohio—Columbus
Oklahoma—Oklahoma City
Oregon—Salem
Pennsylvania—Harrisburg
Rhode Island—Providence
South Carolina—Columbia

States and Capitals (page 93)

South Dakota—Pierre
Tennessee—Nashville
Texas—Austin
Utah—Salt Lake City
Vermont—Montpelier
Virginia—Richmond
Washington—Olympia

West Virginia—Charleston
Wisconsin—Madison
Wyoming—Cheyenne

Solar System Alphabetical Order (page 115)

Earth
Jupiter
Mars
Mercury
Neptune
Pluto
Saturn
Sun
Uranus
Venus

Habitats Alphabetical Order (page 116)

animals
climate
desert
ecosystem
environment
forest
grassland
marine
plants
tundra

Plants Alphabetical Order (page 117)

flower
leaf
photosynthesis
pollen
root
seed
soil
stem
sunlight
water

Homophones (page 118)

The Lakers beat the Bulls.
I ate the whole pie.

Mary got her hair cut.
Dogs are not allowed in the library.
He knows how to ride a bike.
She had to wait for the next train.

Homophones (page 119)

There is a deer near the pond.
She knew the answer to the question.
Please do not waste time.
I went through the tunnel.
The fish lives in the sea.
Tim rode his bike to the store.

Compound Words (page 120)

checkerboard
drumstick
bathroom
eggplant
homework
moonlight
tablespoon
wallpaper
windmill
applesauce

Compound Words (page 121)

everybody
brainstorm
armchair
doorbell
scarecrow
blackberry
shortstop
weekend
outlaw
railroad

Parts of Speech (page 122)

Nouns
ocean
jacket
heart
sister
gasoline

pencil
window
student

Verbs
frighten
grow
invite
wrote
feel
catch
sweep
study

Adjectives
healthy
happy
lovely
young
enormous
strange
salt
fancy

Syllables (page 123)

Two Syllables
morning
certain
complete
common
almost
hundred
whether
special
person

Three Syllables
paragraph
elephant
banana
computer
important
dinosaur
telephone

creative
delicious

Syllables (page 124)

Four Syllables
activity
magnificent
comprehension
watermelon
geography
America
caterpillar
rhinoceros

Five Syllables
vocabulary
unnecessary
vegetarian
electricity
bibliography
communication
opportunity
hippopotamus

Antonyms (page 125)

kind—cruel
many—few
exterior—interior
asleep—awake
common—rare
happy—sad
loose—tight
part—whole
healthy—sick

Synonyms (page 126)

easy—simple
genuine—real
fast—quick
odor—smell
timid—shy
whole—entire
enormous—gigantic
help—assist
mix—blend

Cursive Handwriting © 2004 Creative Teaching Press